Fairies FOREVER

Fairies at School

Phidal

Do you believe in fairies? Discover the enchanting lives of fairies through this fun-filled sticker book. Complete the games with your reusable stickers. Then use your imagination to create your own stories on the last page.

5 years and up.

© 2005 Phidal Publishing Inc.
Produced and Published by Phidal Publishing Inc.
5740 Ferrier, Montreal, Quebec, Canada H4P 1M7
All rights reserved.
Printed in Malaysia.
www.phidal.com

ISBN: 2-7643-0231-2

Talented Teachers

Young fairies study all types of exciting subjects in fairy school. Can you pair up each talented fairy teacher with the subject that she teaches?

Gardening Teacher

Swimming Teacher

Spell-Casting Teacher

Flying Teacher

Please Be Prepared!

Oops! These little fairies have forgotten some of their dance clothes! Help them whirl and twirl in style by placing your stickers over the right shadows.

Wand Magic

In spell-casting class, these fairies are learning the basics of wand magic. Use your stickers to perform these enchanting tasks.

on and off

open and closed

full and empty

young and old

big and small

Let's Make Music!

The fairies assemble for music class in the heart of the magical forest. Help them play a pretty tune with your stickers.

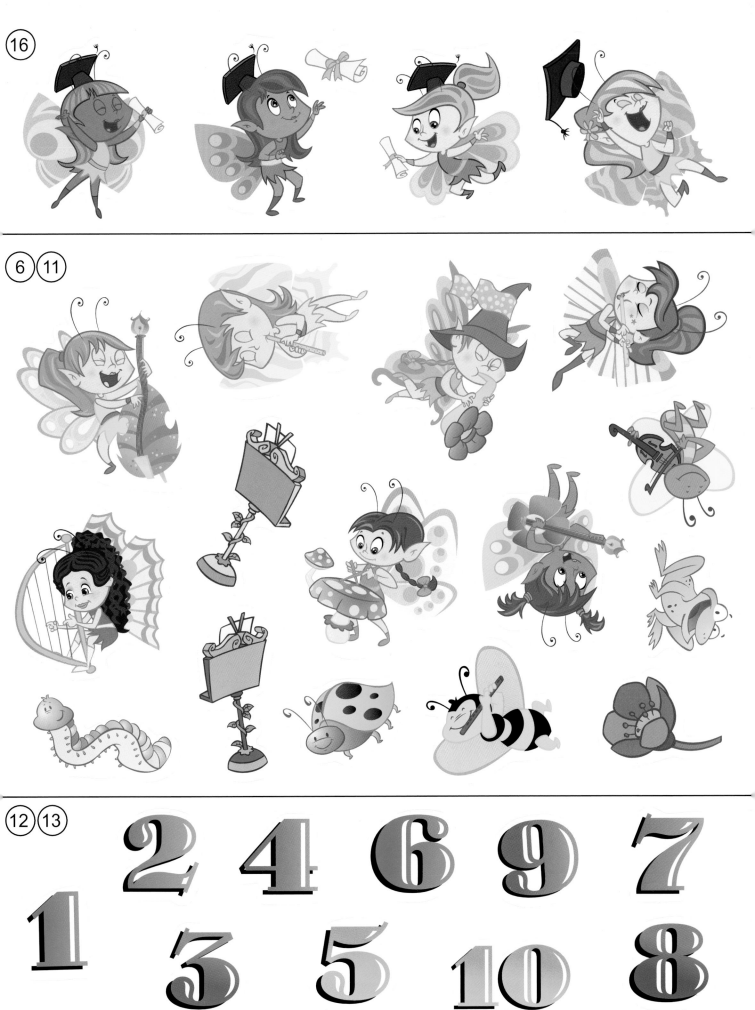

Classroom Counting

A fairy classroom is filled with many supplies. You may even find some of these in your own school! Count and match each object with a number sticker.

hat

bees

inkwells

desks

feathers

dragonflies

apples

books

wands

butterflies

Nature Studies

It is important for young fairies to study nature. Learn about the fairies' surroundings by placing each sticker in the right nature category.

Elements

Water Creatures

Plants

Insects

What's Missing?

It's graduation day for these happy fairies. Can you make the scene below look like the one above with your stickers?